C000271577

What to see i
Boscastle

JIM CASTLING

Bossiney Books · Launceston

Publishers' note

Jim Castling finished writing this book 18 months before the village
he loved was devastated by a flood, and sadly he died within weeks
of the disaster. He would have been immensely proud of the
community's response as it seeks to rebuild – but not in the least
surprised: it is only what he would have expected.

Jim's book was a very personal response to the village, and – except
for one photograph – we have decided to reprint it as it stands
rather than trying to edit it to reflect what is, in any case,
a fast-changing scene.

This reprint 2005
First published 2003 by Bossiney Books Ltd, Langore, Launceston, Cornwall PL15 8LD
www.bossineybooks.com
© 2003 Jim Castling   All rights reserved
ISBN 1-899383-57-3

Acknowledgements
Research: Rod and Anne Knight's *Boscastle Archive*, with contributions by Michael Webber.
The photographs on pages 14 and 15 are reproduced by kind permission of the Royal
Institution of Cornwall. All other photographs are from the publisher's collection
or taken by the author. The map on page 2 is by Graham Hallowell.

Printed in Great Britain by R Booth Ltd, Mabe, Cornwall

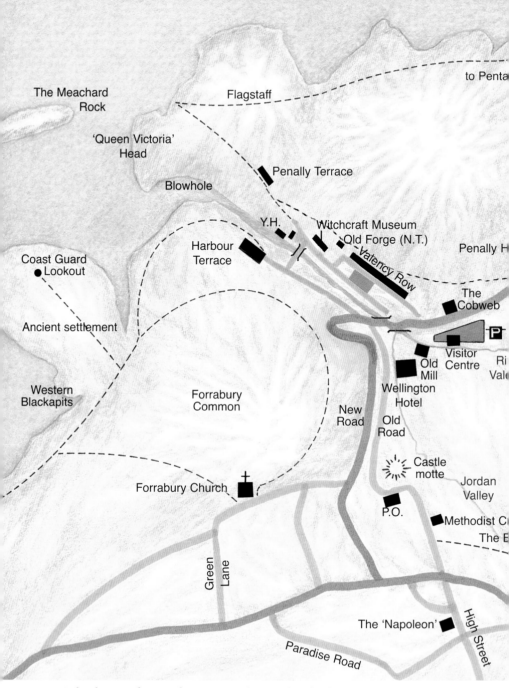

A sketch map of Boscastle, not precisely to scale. The dotted lines represent footpaths, some of which are covered by the walks in this book

Introduction

The first impression you get as you approach Boscastle is a breath-taking view of the coastline as you start to descend, rather as if by aeroplane, along the road from Camelford. The folding countryside suddenly stretches out 175 metres below, with the distant village spilling over the craggy valley. A dramatic backcloth is provided by the glinting sea, while the angular north Cornish coastline stretches away to the north and south. Then, after curving through the magical, dappled light of the beechwood, you begin the final descent down the New Road (it was built in 1875) level with the roofs of the late Victorian villas set precariously on the lip of the Jordan valley.

Crawling around the hairpin bend, with its dramatic glimpse of the harbour, you finally 'land' in Bridge Town, heart of the ancient port.

Boscastle has been a place of welcome since earliest times when its extraordinary natural harbour offered the only refuge between Bude and Padstow from the boisterous sea. At one time it was the bustling centre of trade for a wide area – until the invention of automotive power most goods were carried long distances by sea. When the railway came to nearby Camelford in 1893 the port went into precipitous decline. Since then its main source of income has been tourism.

The view back towards the village from the harbour mouth

Boscastle's attraction derives partly from its catastrophic geology. Set in a steep-sided valley, a natural harbour is formed as the River Valency enters the sea. The land waters are denied direct access by a vast outcrop of hard quartz which reinforces the sea cliffs in their path. That elbow of intervening rock has resisted the erosion of eons and the river has long since made its own way around the obstacle. The 'S' bend that results has proved a blessing, protecting ships from the teasy moods of the sea while at the same time setting a hazardous passage for the unwary sailor.

From very early days the village of Boscastle has comprised three distinct elements, each at a different elevation. First and foremost there is the harbour, consisting of Quay Town and Bridge Town, the source of work and prosperity for earlier communities.

The next level is the medieval core, well up on the steep hillside. In the mid-11th century William de Botterel was granted this small coastal estate in return for his support during the Norman Conquest and he built what became known as 'Bottreaux Castell' on the commanding hillside, inland from the harbour. The village that grew up around it took on the castle's name and eventually became corrupted to 'Boscastle'. This is where the people whose livelihood depended on

4

Just days after the disaster of August 2004, the great clean-up begins

the harbour lived, shopped and worshipped.

Forrabury Common – the third level – was the agricultural land that supported them. It is one of the finest surviving examples of an ancient communal farming system with individual strips or 'stitches'.

Cornwall has always been an important centre for mining. Its tin and copper deposits contributed greatly to Bronze Age technology as far afield as the eastern Mediterranean. The Phoenicians and then the Romans traded for minerals along the Cornish coast for centuries; later, as colonists, the Romans encountered established Iron Age settlements here. Much later, in the Napoleonic era, Cornwall was still the 'most important metalliferous mining centre in Europe'. In more modern times, alumni of the Cornish School of Mines at Camborne have carried their know-how to virtually every important mineral centre in the world.

So Cornwall's long history is characterised by its rich indigenous mineral wealth, and by its people's trading instincts, their ability to mix peacefully with strangers, master the sea, and export goods and technology. These traditions are still enshrined in microcosm in Boscastle today and account for much of its beautiful scenery and special atmosphere.

The Cobweb Inn; the building on this side of it is the pottery

A walk around the harbour area

A brief but fascinating tour of Boscastle starts from the car park. Right opposite the entrance is The Cobweb Inn – a tall, black slate structure with a pyramidal roof, built in the late 17th century. It is now a popular local free house in the best Cornish tradition, but its history reveals an influential role in the port's affairs for three centuries.

Before it became a pub in 1947, it was the warehouse of importers and merchants Bowering & Olde who sold corn, coal, building materials and household items. Harry Bowering arrived from London in 1906, having bought a partnership in W S Hawker's established merchant business. The business was already in decline as a result of the coming of the railways. Hawker committted suicide a few months later.

Hawker had been the third generation owner of Rosevear & Sloggatt, a business that had contributed greatly to the development and prosperity of Boscastle. His father, Claudius Hawker, was the brother of the famous Robert 'Parson' Hawker, vicar of Morwenstow and son-in-law of the first William Sloggatt. With his partner Thomas Pope Rosevear, William Sloggatt founded their merchant business in the Cobweb building at the turn of the 19th century. Most notably they were importers of wines and spirits.

Right next door is Boscastle Pottery where Roger Irving Little has been making his distinctive pots since 1957. On the site of the bakery started by Harry Bowering, Roger Little, working with his wife and son, has established a world-wide reputation for his Mocha-ware. This unique range of pottery is decorated with tree and shrub patterns formed naturally through the capillarity of the glazing.

6

*The Old
Manor House*

*Bridge Town,
site of many
of Boscastle's
harbourside
businesses*

Next to the pottery is the Old Manor House. This still quite elegant Georgian house was once the home of the Lord of the Manor, after his original seat at the top of the village was demolished in 1818. Today it is a popular restaurant specialising in fresh, locally caught fish.

Take the next turning right into Valency Row, the original cobbled high street of Bridge Town, skirting the 'island' of buildings on your left. At the harbour end of the block was a coal warehouse built by Rosevear & Sloggatt. In 1922 Richard Webber, with his two sons Norman and Richard, started a garage and taxi business there. They introduced the first motorbus service out of the village.

Being a port, peopled by sailors and men performing heavy labour, there was always a healthy market for refreshment – at one time there were eighteen pubs in the village. You will pass Robin Cottage on the right, which was once The Robin; then, as the narrow row opens up to gardens on the left, there is The Ship. Once one of Boscastle's most famous pubs, The Ship closed when its two proprietors were conscripted in World War I. Until then, it had for generations been a favourite haunt of sailors, travellers and elements of the gentry. The Reverend R S Hawker was a frequent visitor here.

It is when passing The Ship that Profile Rock, with its uncanny resemblance to Queen Victoria, can first be seen in the distance. The cottage next door is The Brew House, which provided The Ship's vital product. Next door to that is Valency House. Before it last changed hands in 1992 it was a hotel. It is said to have its origins in the 16th century and to this day there is a 'smugglers' hole' in the sitting room,

Valency Row

Rear terrace, left to right: Valency House, The Brew House and the former Ship Inn. Bottom left is the Rocket House, once home of the Life-Saving Apparatus

which has echoes of sea-faring days. It was probably where contraband was stashed. Some believe it may have been a hiding place from pirates or even Napoleonic raiders or, perhaps, a short cut for escaping from them. Valency House was once the home of Thomas Rickard Avery, a local merchant roundly loathed by Parson Hawker who characterised him as 'a notorious wrecker and receiver of contraband'.

Avery was a fierce competitor to Rosevear & Sloggatt in the first half of the 19th century, and between them they controlled the trade of Boscastle. Merchant, tea importer, ship builder and owner, transporter of emigrants and part owner of Delabole Slate Quarry, Avery's interests were wide. But what attracted the greatest opprobrium were his activities as a 'wrecker'. He held a Board of Trade licence for the recovery and disposal rights of the cargoes and remains of ships wrecked along these shores.

During recent excavations for Valency House's garden pond, shards of pottery were found under the lawn which, curiously, were decorated but not glazed. Roger Little, an amateur archaeologist, believes they were pots that had been broken during manufacture. Further research showed that one John Burnard left Barnstaple, then a main English centre of pottery production, with his new bride in 1659 to start a potting business in Boscastle. It must have been very close by.

Sunnyside, next door to Valency House, is the home of the present Harbour Master. The post is largely honorary today: the master is elected by the Boscastle Fishermen's Association, collects dues and is responsible for summoning the Coast Guard in emergencies. The Coast Guard is still an important organisation in Boscastle, with its treacherous coastline and precipitous cliffs. The main task is to respond to calls for help from people in difficulties on the cliffs or beaches, or from swimmers and in-shore sailors in danger. The Boscastle Coast Guard station was established in 1844 in the building now called Olde Carpenter's Shop across the river from the Harbour Master. In 1888 the station was equipped with the Board of Trade's Life Saving Apparatus (LSA) which enabled rescuers to fire a line as far as 500 metres and set up a rescue shuttle from ship to shore by breeches buoy. This equipment was stored in the new 'Rocket House', the red brick building with the sharply pitched roof adjacent to Valency lawn. In early Coast Guard reports there are many stories of dramatic rescues under the most terrifying circumstances.

The small National Trust shop set back from the Harbour Master's house was once the village blacksmith's forge. Before World War I it was connected by a wooden bridge to the former Coast Guard station which had by then been converted into a carpenter's shop. Cart wheels were made there and then bowled over the bridge to the blacksmith where red-hot iron tyres were shrunk onto them in a dramatic display of smoke and sizzle.

The National Trust shop, set back from the Harbour Master's house, was once the village blacksmith's forge

The Harbour Restaurant, with the lime kiln on its right

You will soon pass the great black monolith of the lime kiln where limestone was converted into quicklime. As 'slaked lime' it was used by masons for mortar as well as for the basis of whitewash. The stone from which the kiln is built, black slate patterned with quartz intrusions, is typical Boscastle stone and is the stuff of many of the buildings in the village.

Next you will encounter The Harbour Restaurant, which was at one time the village hall and later, in the 1930s and during World War II, a cinema. The building attached, picturesquely named Bottreaux Court, was a warehouse in the high days of the port. At one stage it was used to store one of the important Boscastle exports, reflected in the bold fascia board lettering plainly seen in Victorian photographs – 'Vivian's Manure Store'.

Mr Vivian, son-in-law of Claudius Hawker, was another Boscastle trader. His speciality business was a by-product of a vital facet of harbour life: horses. They were, of course, the prime means of transport and there were a great many of them. The steepness of the hill demanded that horses pulling loads from the harbour had to be changed and rested at the half-way stage. The sight, sound and the smell of them must have been one of the defining experiences of old Boscastle. The Wellington Hotel ran a daily coach-and-four service to Camelford Station until the outbreak of World War I.

11

The view from the last bridge, with the Youth Hostel on the right. Quite sizeable boats were built in the embrasure past Highwater Cottage on the left

The last bridge over the Valency before the harbour. Harbour Light, the picturesque shop, is behind, alongside the Coastal Path

Passing by the last bridge over the Valency, you will enter a small square with the Museum of Witchcraft on the right (part of this building was once fish cellars). First set up on the Isle of Man in 1952, the museum was brought to Boscastle by Cecil Williamson in 1961. Graham King bought it from him at midnight on 31 October 1996. It is believed to be the largest of its kind in the world.

The Harbour Light, the picturesque shop with the swooping roof on the other side of the square, was a pig-house until Norman Webber converted it into the boutique and ice cream shop. It is one of the most photographed buildings in North Cornwall.

Behind the shop is the Youth Hostel, a favourite holiday centre for the not-necessarily-so-young. The present building dates from 1875. Converted into a youth hostel in 1962, it had been known as 'Palace Stables' and was home to many of the port's horses. The title 'palace' derives from fish-salting buildings, known as 'fish palaces', one of which must have occupied the site. Pilchard fishing was a vital industry in Cornwall: in addition to their value as food, pilchards were important for their oil. They were layered with salt in barrels as soon as they were landed. Heavy weights were placed on them to press out the oil.

The Lively *of Bideford, unloading wool in 1905*

As many as 300 ships a year were handled in the port, each carrying an average of 80 to 100 tons burden. Incoming goods ranged from coal to wines and spirits; outgoing would normally be slate and limestone from the many quarries in the district.

Incoming sailing ships anchored outside the harbour, some tying up to Meachard rock to wait for the right tide conditions before entering. They were met by the 30ft long hobble boat, crewed by nine oarsmen. They towed the ships into the harbour, seeing them safely to their mooring, for a fee of 3 pence per ton of cargo carried. If the sea was running high, the hobble boat could not venture past Penally Point without being swamped, but if a ship passed the Point coming in and the hobble boat was not there to meet her, she was in danger of being smashed against the rocks of Willapark. Always anxious to get under way, ships would expect to enter on one tide and leave on the next.

Although the business of the harbour dropped catastrophically after the arrival of the railway at Camelford in 1893, the *Francis Beddoe* continued to ply from Boscastle well into the 20th century. In 1916 she brought a cargo of coal assigned to merchant Daniel Ward, who had a dispute with the unloading crew. He became so irked with their attitude that he swore it would be the last cargo he would bring into Boscastle by sea. It seems much more likely that German U-boats in the Bristol Channel were the true reason for transferring his business to the railway. However, it certainly was the last cargo ship ever to be unloaded in Boscastle harbour.

A variety of craft in the harbour in the 1890s, including two sailing coasters

Penally Terrace on the right, with a 'fish palace' behind

The fish palace behind Penally Terrace

Climb up the path and you will shortly pass Penally Terrace. Today the cottages that make up the terrace are greatly prized by holiday makers for their commanding view over the harbour. They were homes of fishermen and port workers within living memory. The line of buildings behind them was another old 'fish palace' where the latest catches were salted and the nets were mended.

Continuing along the path to Penally Point, notice the main Cornwall Coastal Path that branches up towards the flagstaff (see page 30 for this walk). Carry on up to the slate plateau at the foot of the final climb to the top of the Queen's Head. The views at this point are

This remarkable example of folded rock strata is found on the slate plateau at the harbour mouth. Imagine the forces required to do this to rock!

spectacular north-eastwards where the coastline makes its jagged, craggy way to Bude and beyond. The listening antennae of the 'Composite Signals Organisation' show their white discs at Morwenstow and, beyond that, on a clear day you can make out Hartland Point. On very clear days Lundy Island stands out strikingly in the channel. In the middle distance is High Cliff, the highest coastal cliff in the country at 223 metres.

The huge outcrop of folded and inverted strata is witness to the volcanic activities that melted and folded the slate. It was laid down millions of years earlier as sediment at the bottom of a long disappeared ocean. Boscastle and the Valency Valley are set astride a rift between two geological systems: one Devonian, about 400 million years old, and the other Carboniferous, around 300-320 million years old. Molten lava seeped through the sediments on the sea bed, melting the layers and converting them to slate. Later volcanic activity melted the slate again and thrust it into folds, forming the astonishing shapes seen today. Molten silica was forced under tremendous pressure into fissures in the slate layers, forming the white, quartz intrusions that so characterise Boscastle rock.

'Seagulls' – the low white building on the left – was once a manganese mill and Harbour Terrace, the tall building behind, was formerly a warehouse known as 'Fox's Cellars'

For the rest of the harbour walk, go back to the harbour square and cross over to the south side. The low building called 'Seagulls', half-left as you cross the bridge, was converted from a carpenter's shop soon after World War II, but its history goes back a good deal further – it was also a manganese mill in the early 19th century.

Moving right, the outstanding building in the harbour on the left, Harbour Terrace, is four separate houses today. Before 1887, it was known as 'Fox's Cellars' and was a warehouse; at one time salt was stored there. It is thought that fish-smoking was carried out in another building alongside.

Walking down towards the quay, you'll pass Highwater Cottage. Just past it, notice the embrasure in the cliff alongside the path. This is where ship-building was carried on by Thomas Rickard Avery. It is hard to imagine today but quite sizeable ships were built, tucked into that space. Ships owned by Avery, *Dew Drop* and *Spring Flower*, were engaged in the flourishing emigration business in the 1820s and continued until the 1850s. They carried up to 180 passengers and plied from Boscastle and Padstow to Quebec, St John's and New York. Some passengers may have been reluctant emigrants, encouraged to move to distant shores so that the parish no longer had to support them financially.

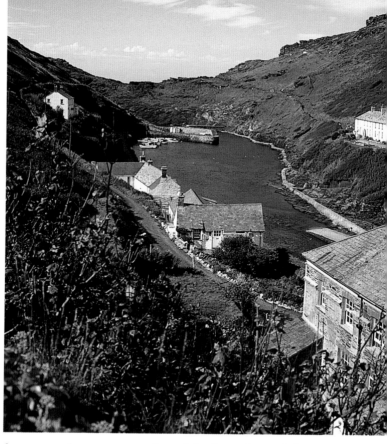

Looking west along the south side of the harbour from the footpath at the hairpin bend

Near the harbour mouth you can see the original granite and slate quay curling backwards to protect moored vessels and afford access for loading and unloading. This famous quay was built for Sir Richard Grenville in 1584, to replace one dating from 1547: construction of the pier involved vertical slates, evidently loosely packed end-ways on to the water. There is good empirical science in this system, which was state-of-the art at the time. As waves hit the walls, the force is dissipated through the gaps, thereby greatly reducing the impact on the structure. Solid walls, even granite, take the full force of the waves and soon start to shift and break up.

Climb up the steep steps past the pier to gain a magnificent view of the harbour entrance and the open sea past Meachard Rock. High up to the left, Willapark dominates the skyline, topped with its Coast Guard lookout. The tower was built by Tom Avery early in the 19th century, originally, it is believed, as a 'folly'. It later became the Coast Guard observation station, with the revenue men on the watch for undeclared goods and liquor entering port.

The famous Boscastle blowhole in action. Its performance can vary according to the prevailing weather conditions

Standing on this slate platform, polished over the centuries by the feet of fishermen, sailors and port officials, you can see deep, square grooves in the surface which housed the foundations of huts from which port business was supervised. Below, at about high-tide level, is a square pool cut into the rock, which used to be a storage tank for shellfish to keep them alive and fresh (and safe from theft) until sold. Right opposite, at water level, is that popular Boscastle feature – the blowhole. At an hour on either side of low tide, when swell conditions are right, pressure builds up in the inner chamber within the rock, which then forces a jet of water across the harbour mouth with a loud whoosh!

Now retrace your steps back to Bridge Town. As you leave the harbour entrance, take a last look at the outer pier on the opposite side of the harbour. It was built much later than the main pier, in the early 19th century; another enterprise of the ubiquitous Tom Avery, who formed an uneasy working arrangement with his rival, T P Rosevear. They constructed this outer pier as extra protection for their docked ships. It was severely damaged by a drifting German mine soon after World War II and it subsequently disintegrated in a storm. It was not reconstructed until 1962, when stone saved from the Old Laira Bridge at Plymouth was used to replace that washed away by the sea.

Willapark, with the Lookout, seen from just opposite the blowhole

The Old Mill, with its decorative waterwheel

Walking back, you will soon have the end of your harbour tour in sight as The Wellington Hotel and the Old Mill come into view. The mill, like the lime kiln, was a crucial amenity for harbour trade and was used to make flour from local and imported grain. The overshot water wheel seen today is purely decorative and was installed by a recent Boscastle trader, electrician David Turner, in the 1980s. The original one, with all its interior machinery, was sold off for scrap before World War II; it ground its last flour in 1935.

Finally, you will arrive at the most imposing building in the village, The Wellington Hotel. At around 400 years in age, it is one of the oldest coaching inns in North Cornwall. The Duke of Wellington probably never set foot in it, but the inn took its name as a tribute to the great man on his death in 1852.

It has certainly played host to a number of other celebrities, however: Edward VII took a party there; Sir Henry Irving, the first knighted thespian, rested there; Thomas Hardy stayed during his visit to refurbish St Juliot's Church – the lamps in the Long Bar were designed and donated by Hardy on completion of his work.

Wing Commander Guy Gibson, VC, hero of the Möhne Dam raid, also stayed there at one stage in his career when he made inspection visits to RAF Davidstow. His signature is in the hotel register of the day.

The historic Wellington Hotel, in origin some 400 years old, and one of the oldest coaching inns in Cornwall

The Lookout, a famous feature of the north Cornwall coast

Outer tour of Boscastle

On this walk you can look at more of Boscastle village and trace the domestic lives of the local people, most of whom spent their working lives at the harbour. You can also give the Lookout closer inspection.

Start on the south side of the harbour this time, opposite the mill, and walk back past the main pier, then up the rock steps and on up the steepish path to the Lookout. The mouth of the harbour soon recedes; Meachard Rock becomes a more dominant element of the landscape and there is an excellent view of the coastline.

At the top, skirt Eastern Blackapits, taking care not to lean too heavily on the wire – it is 60 metres straight down to the rocks. As you toil up to the Lookout, notice ditches and mounds under the brambles on the falling ground between you and the harbour. This is the site of an extensive ancient settlement, and it is quite likely that the people who lived here traded with the Romans and Phoenicians.

Reaching the top at last, you stand alongside one of the most recognisable, salient features of the north Cornish coast. Refurbished by The National Trust, the lookout tower has been placed at the disposal of the National Coastwatch Institution as one of a chain of vantage points from which to keep a continuing daylight watch over British in-shore waters.

The stitches, an ancient strip-farming system, now owned by The National Trust, but still rented to tenants from nearby farms

Looking across the small bay and Western Blackapits, a huge stone wall is clearly visible on top of the cliff. It is the site of 'California', one of the many cliff-edge slate quarries in the district. Men were suspended perilously on ropes to hack their way into the slate seams. It is said that they soon got used to the height and were pleased to be spared the tedious business of disposing of the spoil, which fell harmlessly into the sea.

If you look further to your left, inland, you can see St Symphorian's Church (more familiarly known as Forrabury Church) on the horizon and, in between, cultivated strips. These strips comprise Forrabury Common which covers about 80 acres and has forty individual 'stitches' of land set out in the same pattern that has been used certainly since the 17th century.

The stitch system soon becomes more evident as you walk further along. Originally each about an acre in size, most of the stitches are curved slightly to facilitate ploughing. They were owned by individuals or syndicates until they were gradually bought up by the Lord of the Manor, although they were still rented to villagers. Between Lady Day and Michaelmas they became common grazing land. The tradition is that every householder in Forrabury had rights to the stitches. In 1955 most of them were acquired by The National Trust when it purchased the harbour.

When you reach Forrabury Church it is worth spending a few minutes here – you can enter by the back gate from the common. A Norman church originally occupied the site, but the building was reconstructed in 1867 to provide more seating. The churchyard has a number of ancient slate grave stones, the carving still relatively unworn by wind and weather. And it is here that you can identify many of the family names still represented in the village.

As you leave, there is an ancient Celtic cross half-way down the green to your right. Celtic crosses are to be found all over Cornwall, many carved in intricate designs in the unyielding granite. This one, like so many others, latterly served as a gatepost.

The Church of St Symphorian, Forrabury

An ancient Celtic cross, now standing just outside Forrabury Church

Looking down High Street, the original heart of the old village

Take a short, brisk walk to the next key element of the village: Paradise, Mount Pleasant and the Jordan Valley. Who could resist it? Turning right from the church, the road bends left by the football pitch and Green Lane continues for about 400 metres until it reaches the main road to Tintagel. Turn left and walk for about 100 metres and cross over by a grassy triangle with huge lace-cap hydrangea plants. At this point you enter Paradise Road, the topmost, southern-most boundary of the village.

Most of the buildings for the first 200 metres are new but soon, on the right, is Paradise House, largely hidden at first by holm oak trees in its drive. It is a small but delightful manor house built around 1820 by Richard Benoke, of a then well-known Boscastle family. It was later owned by Richard Scott, who is thought to have added the imposing tower to The Wellington Hotel.

Pass Paradise Farm on the right, whose working lands spread across an expanse of the south side of the village and include some of the Forrabury Common stitches. You'll soon reach the cross roads where the ancient village originally started. Turn left down High Street. It is a fairly steep descent.

Not all that long ago this short street was a bustling, busy shopping centre. What is today St Christopher's Hotel was once Providence

The Napoleon Inn, which is reputed to be one of the oldest pubs in Cornwall

House, a hotel which later became a general store. Well within living memory there were other shops – a butcher's, a cobbler's, another general store, a chemist's, a draper's and yet a further general store on the south corner.

One remaining hostelry that is still a great favourite both with locals and visitors is The Napoleon Inn. In 1807 the landlord was the local recruiting officer who helped raise forces to stem a threatened invasion by Bonaparte. Many believe this to be the origin of its name, but the first recorded licensee was William Bone and it is possible that his name became corrupted to the Emperor's famous nickname 'Boney'. Boney or Bonney is a not uncommon name in these parts. Indeed, one of the family emigrated to America to produce a notorious descendant, William Bonney, otherwise known as 'Billy the Kid'.

Cottages in Fore Street

Crossing the main road from Camelford, continue down the even steeper hill of Fore Street into the medieval core of the village. On the left corner is Bottreaux Surgery, occupying the site of the Boscastle Sheep Market founded by Royal Charter. It was in continuous use for centuries, right up until the 1960s.

Shops and businesses continued here until relatively modern times: a blacksmith's, another inn, curiously named 'Mumpers' (on the other side of the old sheep market) and North Cornwall Stores, which closed in 1970. The last business to operate in this area was Cowlings, a butcher's shop and slaughter house which closed in 1971. The name 'Cowlings' is still to be seen on the fan light over the front door.

The village hall on the left occupies the site of the old St James's Chapel, known to have been there in 1400 and thought to have been the private chapel to the castle. Notice the delightfully jumbled line of cottages on the left, especially the Old Post House, an irresistible magnet to photographers. Further down on the right, passing the original village school, is the imposing Methodist Church. A church was erected here in 1800 by T P Rosevear in gratitude for his ship being saved from a French privateer's attack in the Bristol Channel; the present church was built by Rosevear's son in 1825.

You then sweep on past the beautiful cottage 'Smugglers' on the left, said to be the oldest building in Boscastle and probably built from stone salvaged from the ruined castle. The roof timbers were salvaged from a wrecked ship.

Now, finally, you reach the site of the original Bottreaux Castle. Opposite Smugglers is a small path which leads up to the grassy motte, where Botterel's fortress commanded the valley. It was built between 1080 and 1117 but few facts are known about it. When John Hender bought the manor in 1575 the castle was already in ruins; in 1796 a visitor recorded that there were no remains then. From the motte there is a pleasant prospect down the valley to the harbour village. The River Jordan runs through on the right to join the Valency under the bridge by the harbour. It may be that the valley below the castle was cultivated into gardens, giving rise to the name Jordan, a corruption of the French *jardin*.

Below the War Memorial Fore Street becomes Dunn Street. The Post Office on the left was once another chapel, built by the later merchant Jabez Brown; it closed in 1933. Two pubs, the Commercial and Dolphin Inns, thrived along here. There was also the village lock-up.

Carry on down into Old Road, passing Pillar House with its formidable pine columns (originally ships' timbers). Just short of the Wellington Hotel, you pass the attractive line of red stone cottages, Marine Terrace. These were built around 1844 to house coast guards.

Pause for a moment and look up to the impressively turreted 'Valley View', the lower of the Victorian villas that line the New Road approach to the harbour. In many ways these impressive houses epitomise the sea change of livelihood for Boscastle from a working port to a tourism centre and holiday venue. They were completed in 1889, just in time for the opening of the railway at Camelford.

The motte of the Norman castle, seen from near Forrabury Church

The view as you approach the flagstaff – perhaps the best view of the harbour and well worth the climb. From the highest point here you can see Boscastle in relation to the coastline, which diminishes away south to a distant view, in exceptionally clear weather, of The Rumps on Pentire Glaze

Cliff-top walk

Start from the north (right) side of the harbour. Instead of going straight on to Profile Rock, take the steep steps up on the right towards the flagstaff – the continuation of the Cornish Coastal Path. It is worth the climb and, on reaching the flagstaff, affords perhaps the best view of the harbour. It is high enough, too, to see Boscastle in relation to the coastline. From the flagstaff it is a fairly short distance north to Pentargon, an enticing beach which, since a landslip in living memory, became inaccessible except to the experienced rock climber.

At Pentargon Bay take the National Trust path back to the Bude road, where the kissing gate gives onto the road alongside the entrance to Penally House. This elegant villa was built by William Sloggatt, partner of Thomas Rosevear. It fell into near derelict condition until the present owners lovingly restored it during the late 1990s.

Immediately past the drive entrance is a huge gate leading to a path running just below Penally House. This is a public footpath but called The Private Road, or 'Green Cut', and runs for 400 metres or so down to the harbour. Built by Sloggatt to connect his house, his warehouse (The Cobweb) and the harbour, it was his own private access route. It is now a beautiful walk offering fine views of the village and the harbour. The Private Road ends by Penally Terrace, the conspicuous line of cottages overlooking the harbour.

The Valency valley in early Spring

St Juliot Church, an alternative destination on a slightly longer walk

Inland walk

This walk goes inland from the car park and up the Valency Valley. After about 1.5 km there is a wooden bridge over the stream and a signpost. (If you have plenty of time, straight on will ultimately bring you to St Juliot Church, the famous first assignment for the young architect Thomas Hardy where the rector's daughter Emma Gifford caught his eye.) The recommended walk takes you across the river and up the path signed towards Minster Church.

Climbing up through the enchanting woods you will see the valley stretching out below. Eventually you will arrive at Minster Church which occupies the site of a medieval monastery.

Minster Church, a most evocative place: the church has an unusual (for Cornwall) pointed, saddle-back tower, and is set in dense, silent woodland

After the church, turn right along the road that runs higher alongside it, past Home Farm, to a small crossroads with a charming dolls' house cottage on its corner. Take the downward road on the right and descend steeply for 300 metres to where the road takes a 90° turn to the left. At this point climb over the stile, continuing straight on across the field, taking the public footpath to the village.

You will walk diagonally left across the meadow, and the dipping path then follows a stream leading to a cottage, 'The Butts'. Its small pond normally has geese and muscovy ducks which may hiss at you, but they they will let you pass in front of The Butts to take the path uphill through the gateway.

As the path curves upwards, notice on the left one of the very few, and evidently completely healthy, remaining wych elm trees – a truly magnificent and nostalgic sight. Almost immediately you will find yourself back on Fore Street, opposite the church hall, and from there it is a short step back to the village.